Date: 5/13/14

J BIO UNDERTAKER
Scheff, Matt,
Undertaker /

UNDERTAKER

BY MATT SCHEFF

Printed in the United States of America,
North Mankato, Minnesota
102013
012014

 THIS BOOK CONTAINS AT LEAST 10% RECYCLED MATERIALS.

Editor: Chrös McDougall
Series Designer: Jake Nordby

Photo Credits: Mike Lano Photojournalism, cover, 1, 8-9, 30 (top); Mel Evans/ AP Images, cover (background), 1 (background); Paul Abell/AP Images for WWE Corp., 4-5; Matt Roberts/Zuma Press/Icon SMI, 6-7, 10-11, 15 (inset), 24-25, 28-29, 31; Seth Poppel/Yearbook Library, 6 (inset); Chris Carlson/AP Images, 12-13; Alexandre Pona/CITYFILES/Icon SMI, 14-15; Heather Rousseau/ Splash News/Newscom, 16-17, 22; SI1 WENN Photos/Newscom, 18-19, 20 (inset); Glyn Kirk/Action Plus/Icon SMI, 20-21; Jacob Langston/MCT/Newscom, 23; Rick Scuteri/AP Images, 25 (inset), 26-27, 30 (middle), 30 (bottom)

Library of Congress Control Number: 2013945679

Cataloging-in-Publication Data

Scheff, Matt.
  Undertaker / Matt Scheff.
    p. cm. -- (Pro wrestling superstars)
Includes index.
ISBN 978-1-62403-141-0
1. Undertaker, 1965- --Juvenile literature. 2. Wrestlers--United States-- Biography--Juvenile literature. 1. Title.
796.812092--dc23
[B]

2013945679

CONTENTS

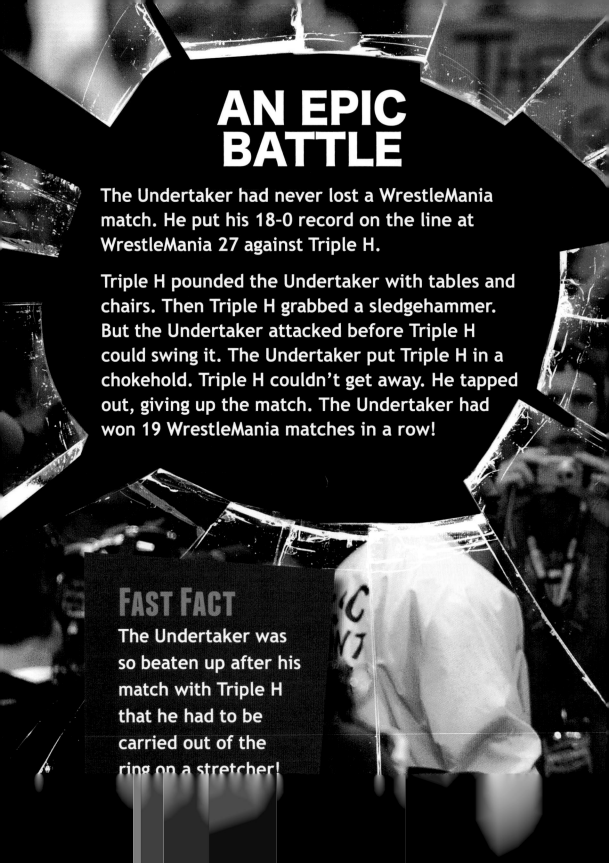

AN EPIC BATTLE

The Undertaker had never lost a WrestleMania match. He put his 18-0 record on the line at WrestleMania 27 against Triple H.

Triple H pounded the Undertaker with tables and chairs. Then Triple H grabbed a sledgehammer. But the Undertaker attacked before Triple H could swing it. The Undertaker put Triple H in a chokehold. Triple H couldn't get away. He tapped out, giving up the match. The Undertaker had won 19 WrestleMania matches in a row!

FAST FACT

The Undertaker was so beaten up after his match with Triple H that he had to be carried out of the ring on a stretcher!

The Undertaker manhandles
Triple H at WrestleMania 27.

Calaway in high school

Calaway has always been a fierce competitor.

BEFORE THE UNDERTAKER

The Undertaker's real name is Mark William Calaway. He was born March 24, 1965, in Houston, Texas. Calaway was always a good athlete. He played basketball and football in high school. He went on to play basketball for Angelina College and for Texas Wesleyan University (TWU).

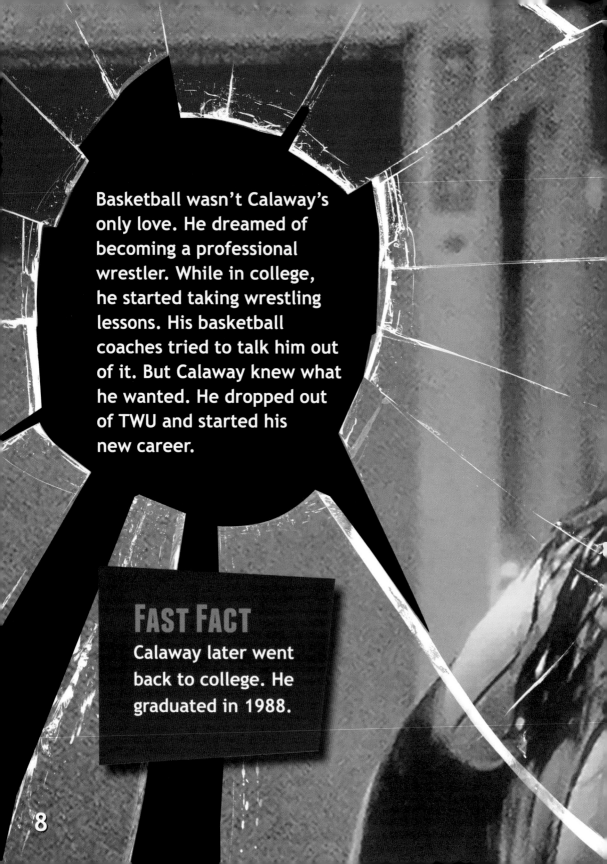

Basketball wasn't Calaway's only love. He dreamed of becoming a professional wrestler. While in college, he started taking wrestling lessons. His basketball coaches tried to talk him out of it. But Calaway knew what he wanted. He dropped out of TWU and started his new career.

FAST FACT

Calaway later went back to college. He graduated in 1988.

8

Calaway turned to professional wrestling during college.

9

Calaway began his career in several small wrestling leagues. He used many names. He started out as Texas Red. He also wrestled as Master of Pain and the Punisher. In 1989, Calaway signed with World Championship Wrestling. His new name was Mean Mark Callous. Callous was a heel. Fans loved to boo him.

FAST FACT

In 1989, Calaway beat wrestling legend Jerry Lawler to win his first championship.

The Undertaker and Shawn Michaels prepare to battle at WrestleMania 25.

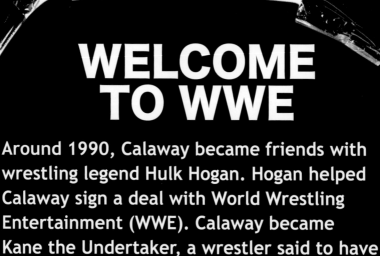

WELCOME TO WWE

Around 1990, Calaway became friends with wrestling legend Hulk Hogan. Hogan helped Calaway sign a deal with World Wrestling Entertainment (WWE). Calaway became Kane the Undertaker, a wrestler said to have returned from the dead. He wore a trench coat and dark clothing. He pretended that he couldn't feel any pain. He would "no-sell" his opponent's moves. That means that he pretended not to feel anything.

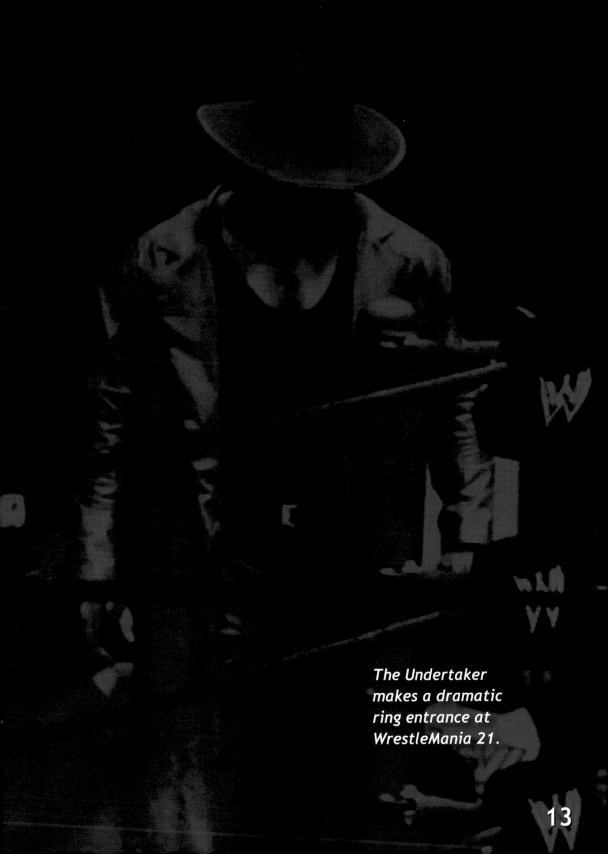

The Undertaker makes a dramatic ring entrance at WrestleMania 21.

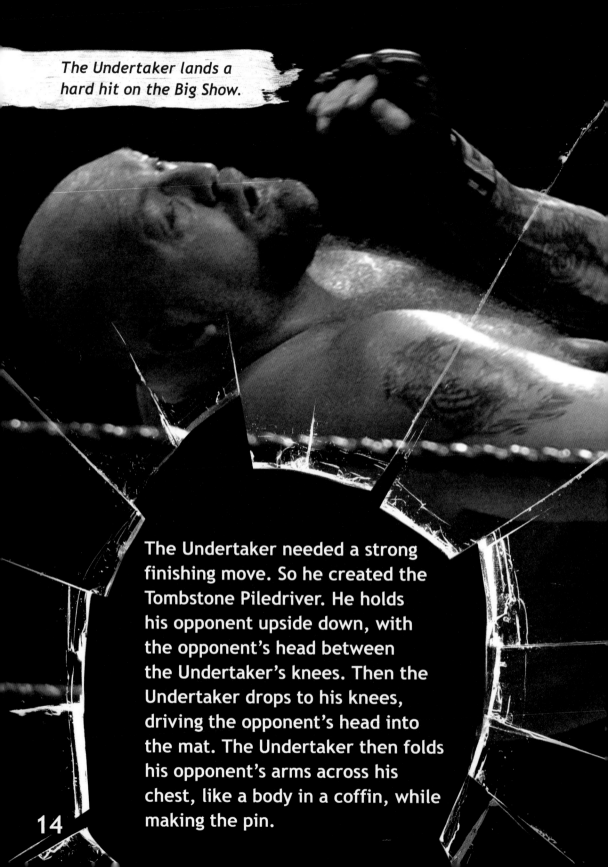

The Undertaker needed a strong
finishing move. So he created the
Tombstone Piledriver. He holds
his opponent upside down, with
the opponent's head between
the Undertaker's knees. Then the
Undertaker drops to his knees,
driving the opponent's head into
the mat. The Undertaker then folds
his opponent's arms across his
chest, like a body in a coffin, while
making the pin.

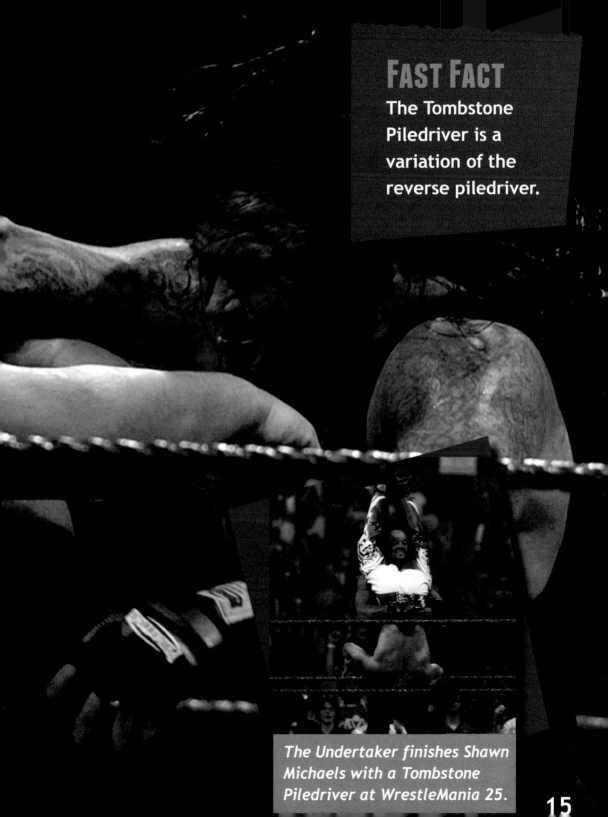

The Undertaker finishes Shawn Michaels with a Tombstone Piledriver at WrestleMania 25.

15

The Undertaker was a hit. He made his first WrestleMania appearance in 1991. He used a Tombstone Piledriver to take down "Superfly" Jimmy Snuka. It was the first in a long series of WrestleMania victories.

The Undertaker strikes fear into his opponents.

The Undertaker prepares himself before entering the ring.

FAST FACT

The Undertaker didn't lose a single match from December 1991 to September 1993!

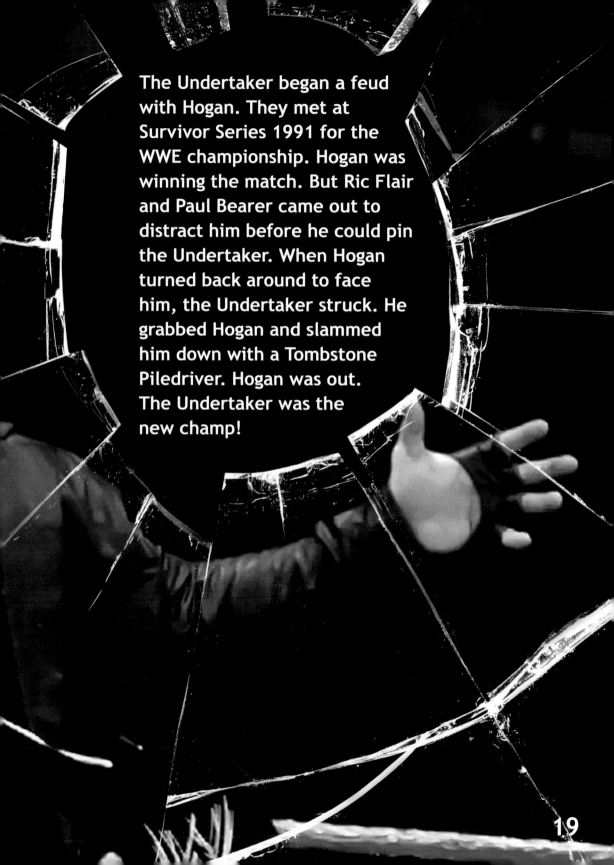

The Undertaker began a feud with Hogan. They met at Survivor Series 1991 for the WWE championship. Hogan was winning the match. But Ric Flair and Paul Bearer came out to distract him before he could pin the Undertaker. When Hogan turned back around to face him, the Undertaker struck. He grabbed Hogan and slammed him down with a Tombstone Piledriver. Hogan was out. The Undertaker was the new champ!

BUILDING A LEGEND

The Undertaker remained one of WWE's biggest stars throughout the 1990s. He spent time as a heel and a baby face. He had feuds with Ted DiBiase, Mankind, and Shawn Michaels. He even feuded with a new character called Kane. WWE told fans that Kane was the Undertaker's younger brother.

Kane and the Undertaker have had many famous battles.

The Undertaker battles with Mankind.

FAST FACT

Kane claimed that he had been burned and scarred in a fire that the Undertaker had set.

21

The Undertaker shows off his world heavyweight championship belt.

FAST FACT

Calaway has four children, one boy and three girls.

The Undertaker was also a successful tag-team wrestler. He won tag-team belts with Steve Austin, the Big Show, the Rock, and Kane. But the real story was the Undertaker's WrestleMania record. In 2002, he pinned Ric Flair to improve to 10-0 all time. Fans wondered how long the streak would last.

The Undertaker takes down Edge at WrestleMania 24.

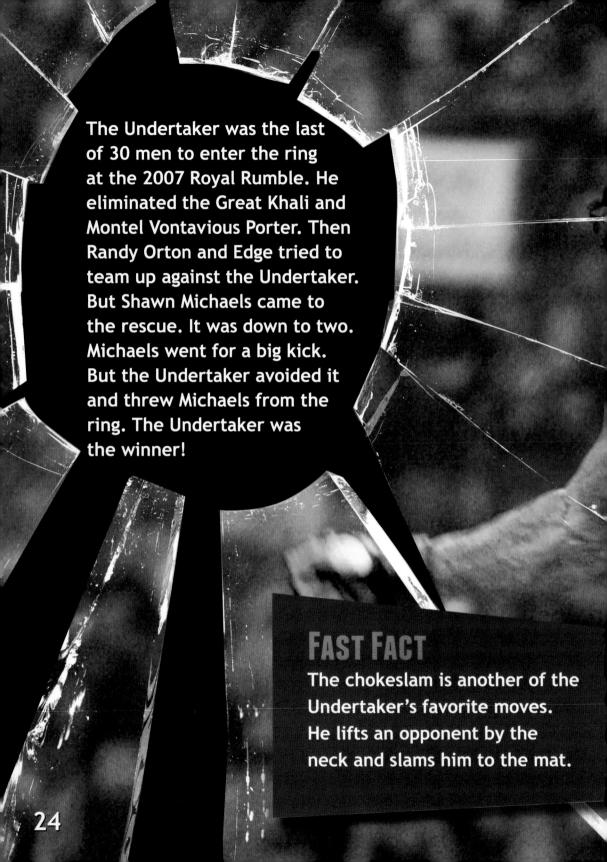

The Undertaker was the last of 30 men to enter the ring at the 2007 Royal Rumble. He eliminated the Great Khali and Montel Vontavious Porter. Then Randy Orton and Edge tried to team up against the Undertaker. But Shawn Michaels came to the rescue. It was down to two. Michaels went for a big kick. But the Undertaker avoided it and threw Michaels from the ring. The Undertaker was the winner!

FAST FACT

The chokeslam is another of the Undertaker's favorite moves. He lifts an opponent by the neck and slams him to the mat.

The Undertaker flies at Shawn Michaels at WrestleMania 25.

The Undertaker throws Shawn Michaels over the ropes at WrestleMania 26.

The Undertaker puts the hurt on Shawn Michaels at WrestleMania 26.

STILL GOING STRONG

In 2010, the Undertaker faced Shawn Michaels at WrestleMania 26. Many fans consider it one of the best matches ever. The two battled hard in and out of the ring. The Undertaker hit Michaels with a chokeslam and two Tombstone Piledrivers to finally end it. The win was his eighteenth straight at WrestleMania!

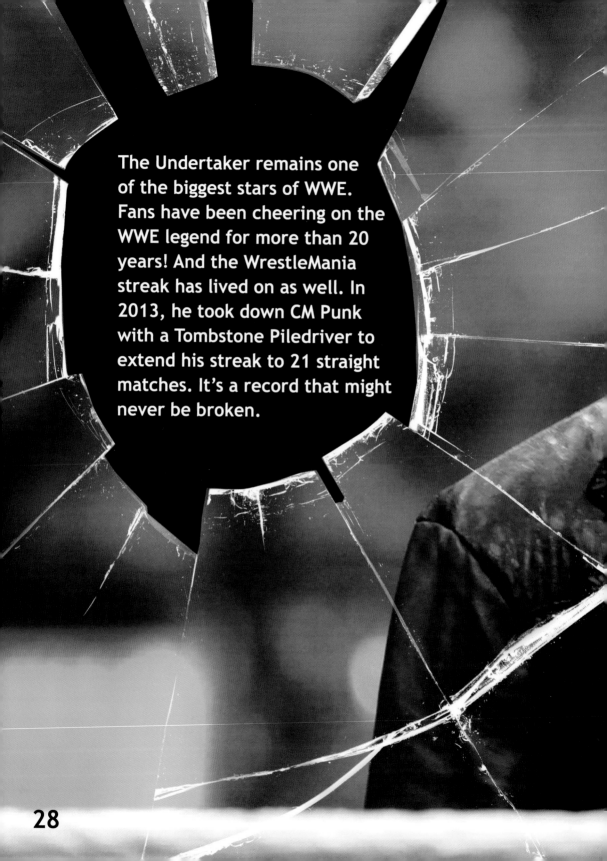

The Undertaker remains one of the biggest stars of WWE. Fans have been cheering on the WWE legend for more than 20 years! And the WrestleMania streak has lived on as well. In 2013, he took down CM Punk with a Tombstone Piledriver to extend his streak to 21 straight matches. It's a record that might never be broken.

The Undertaker mentally prepares to face Triple H at WrestleMania 27.

1965
Mark William Calaway is born on March 24 in Houston, Texas.

1984
Calaway wrestles in his first professional match under the name Texas Red.

1986
Calaway leaves college to pursue wrestling full time.

1990
Calaway signs with WWE and becomes Kane the Undertaker.

1991
The Undertaker wrestles in his first WrestleMania match, defeating "Superfly" Jimmy Snuka.

2001
The Undertaker and Kane team up to win the world tag-team championship.

2007
The Undertaker wins the Royal Rumble.

2013
The Undertaker pins CM Punk for his twenty-first WrestleMania victory in a row.

GLOSSARY

baby face
A wrestler whom fans view as a good guy.

feud
An intense, long-lasting conflict between wrestlers.

finishing move
A powerful move that a wrestler uses to finish off an opponent.

heel
A wrestler whom fans view as a villain.

legend
Somebody who has been very famous for a long time.

no-sell
To pretend not to feel an opponent's strike.

undertaker
The director of a funeral home, now known as a funeral director.

INDEX